CHANGE YOUR WORLD ONE WORD AT A TIME

How the way you speak creates your life

David Firth

Firth has split the atom with this small and explosive book about words and their huge creative leverage... read this, and all your communication will increase in power.

Steve Chandler
Author of *Time Warrior*

ACKNOWLEDGEMENTS

To Stephen for the BOLD work

To Charrise for the Liberation Conversations

To Emre, Melinda and Ricardo for being brave enough to open the space

To Patrick for the fitness being realized

To Mum for the birth of everything

To Steve for having me darken the page – this book would not be here now were it not for your ability to ask a very simple question

To all of you

Thank You.

PREFACE

Before the first word is written, there is the white page. Before the first word is spoken, there is silence. (And before the Big Bang?).

My life has been immersed in the astonishing power of words since the time when, to my then crushing embarrassment, my Elementary Grade Headmaster had me read out to the assembled school a short composition I had written about rain. Fast forward through my life to my English Language & Literature degree from Oxford University, to six years of writing and performing in theater, and on to twenty years of consulting and coaching – a profession that occurs nowhere else than in language (for how all this has profound implications for how we experience and grow business organizations, see my next book: *The New Language of Leadership*).

Truly, if you had the patience, I could sit with you all day discussing the beauty of phrase, rhythm, pace and the brilliance of how character can be expressed in iambic pentameter. Really, I could. But, honestly, none of that matters.

All I need you to understand right now is that the next word you speak could change your life.

CHANGE YOUR WORLD ONE WORD AT A TIME

How the way you speak creates your life

Then, suddenly, I knew not how or where or when, my brain felt the impact of another mind, and I awoke to language, to knowledge of love, to the usual concepts of nature, of good and evil! I was actually lifted from nothingness to human life.

Helen Keller

Saying is inventing.

Samuel Beckett, *Molloy*

So shall my word be that goes out from my mouth; it shall not return to me empty, but it shall accomplish that which I purpose, and shall succeed in the thing for which I sent it.

Isiah 55:11

WORDS ARE SELF-EXPRESSION

We are all of us poets, and the expression of something as big as our lives and what we are up to demands a 'fierce poetry'.

Some of that comes from a new understanding of what our 'ordinary' words can mean and some of it comes from saying what we truly want to say.

Expression is a word we use often in every day talk, but comes from an old Latin verb exprimere, which originally meant 'to press out, to express.'

Like a toothpaste tube, so many of our words shoot out without effort or consideration. Getting the last value from the tube, however, requires an expression, a pressing out, an intentionality.

We need to recapture a sense of power in our lives through the preciousness of what comes out of our mouths: the birthing of our thoughts and intentions into action.

> *'As long as words are made of breath, and breath made of life'*

Prologue, *Anonymous,* Columbia Pictures 2011

I can change my world one word at a time

How do I do that?

By bringing words – language – back into primacy in our experience, not as descriptors of that experience but as makers of it.

There are two reliable ways to do this.

1. USE WORDS THAT CREATE ACTION

The first way is to help people distinguish something that is currently recognized in academia, and on some esoteric web sites: that there are ways of speaking that will produce action and that there are ways of speaking that don't.

In my theater days I learnt that there are different ways to breathe, and, by being able to access different ways of breathing, I had access to different levels, literally, of performance. Not just 'bigger breaths' that would allow me to get to the end of a line without gasping, but deeper breathing with which I was able to give form to nuances of the character's thinking, emotion and 'inner life'.

Prior to getting that understanding, I thought that breathing was just the automatic thing that went on without me having to think about it. I believe that for 99% of the world, the words we speak are just like breathing: we open our mouths and sounds come out. 'What could be so complicated about that? And don't we have enough talking going on in this noisy world of ours? Just look at the politicians...'

We need access to different ways of speaking in order to bring about different levels of our own performance, different levels of living.

2. USE 'BLOOD AND GUTS' WORDS

The second way I can change the world through language is by unleashing the often hidden meanings of words - connecting them again to their source, to the power they had when they were *made*, to their breath of life - trapped as they have been behind centuries-old layers of meaning-making that have stripped those words of their power.

Because if words are what we have to create our experience, then we need great words, words that move, words that speak up and SPEAK OUT!

> *'I want to sing with blood and guts,*
> *So someone will know that I'm here.*
> *I want to sing with blood and guts*
> *And I want them to sing with me too...'*
>
> Middle Brother, *Blood & Guts*

So: words that make things happen, and words that embody our powerful intentions. That's what we are looking for.

Because action gets born in talking.

No. OUR LIVES get born in talking:

Words are life and death

Then, suddenly, I knew not how or where or when, my brain felt the impact of another mind, and I awoke to language, to knowledge of love, to the usual concepts of nature, of good and evil! I was actually lifted from nothingness to human life.

Helen Keller

In 1882, 19 months into her life, Helen Keller contracted an illness – it might have been scarlet fever or meningitis – which left her blind and deaf. The story of how she emerged from an almost total lack of language into a world of communication, meaning, understanding and connection was made famous in the play and subsequent film *The Miracle Worker*.

The big breakthrough – 'big' being too small a word to describe the nature of the rebirth she describes in the quotation above – came when she suddenly connected the experience of the sign language finger motions her teacher Anne Sullivan was making on her hand with the experience of the water running onto her other hand from a faucet. She 'got' the concept of 'water'. She then, apparently, 'nearly exhausted Sullivan demanding the names of all the other familiar objects in her world'.

She became truly alive in the world. Before language: nothingness (or simply a series of nameless sensations). After language: lights on, meaning, power, thirst for growth (she became the first deaf-blind person to earn a degree), to everything it means to be a human being. A shift from being a helpless passenger in her life into being a creator of it.

This book is about how we can have our own rebirths into a fuller, more powerful, more intentional life by getting a new access to the power of language.

Of words.

Sometimes people don't come back

Everything's going to be OK. There will be no problems! And I am also obliged to tell you that sometimes people don't come back.

My Anesthetist to me, January 27th 2012

This book has a very personal meaning in my life.

I had surgery in January of 2012. A day that began like any other day took a sudden and dramatic turn, and within a few hours I was laid in the pre-op room of the St Lukes Presbyterian hospital in Denver, listening to a very kind woman – whose name, sadly, is now lost to me – telling me about the surgery I was about to undergo. Or at least, her own role in the operation as the anesthetist, which was to make me safely and temporarily dead to the world whilst the surgeon did his work with the scalpels and the machine that goes ping (thank you Monty Python).

Those few moments of my life were all shaped by language. Her job was to tell me about the inevitable success of such an operation, but also – and here her body language and vocal tone changed every so slightly – to communicate a form of legal disclaimer. Anesthesia is a wonderful thing and overwhelmingly successful in just about every occasion. And, sometimes, in very rare instances, patients go under, and then don't resurface.

I suppose she was giving me the chance to say No – 'You know what, I think I've changed my mind' – though there seemed a very limited possibility that they were going to listen to me, having already injected me with a drug 'just designed to relax you!' But what her speaking did strike me with was a vital and very immediate understanding of the impact of words.

I had studied language at the University of Oxford; I had spent six years performing drama around the world crafted by masters such as William Shakespeare and Samuel Beckett: and I had made my life's work consulting to organizations small and large (a profession whose success exists nowhere else except in and through sharing understanding together in language). But I have almost never been as awake to the power of words as I was then, in St Luke's, when I realized that the encroaching darkness might be a permanent one.

Famous last words

Apparently Steve Jobs' last word, on his death bed, was 'Wow!' Let me state for the record that my own 'last words' – I had such little time to think! – were 'Bye, babe'. To my wife.

Thankfully – as you know because you are now reading this – I did not become one of those rare statistics. I came back.

And my real, final, last words are going to be amazingly graceful and inspirational. Or maybe I'll just say 'Bye, babe' again.

Whatever the case, this book is my testament to the beauty, elegance and creative power of words and their impact on the life we want to lead.

Watch 'reality' change!

One day, I saw Werner Erhard on YouTube speaking to an audience at Harvard's Kennedy School of Business. He gives an hour-plus talk answering the question 'What is the source of action?' Being a typically Erhard lecture, you really have to sit with it, because this is as far from 'The Secret Simple Seven Steps to Success!' as you can imagine.

And then towards the end, having developed pretty much a single idea for 50 minutes plus, it's as if Werner suddenly decides to throw in a few quick other ideas before his close. It's a funny change of gear and not what I was expecting, and maybe it was that change of gear throwing me off guard, as it were, that allowed me to hear a sentence that has wrapped itself around the 'fleshy contours of my heart' (as my coach's coach says). Which means that it has changed my life.

A concept that I thought I got before I now realize I have really got. As in Got Got. Got not like "Oh yes, I understand what you are saying, how fascinating!" but got as in 'Got it like a joke'. Meaning straight inside, no filters, everything shifted.

The sentence is:

WHALES DO NOT HAVE TOO MUCH TO DO

Because they don't. And this is not because they are whales and we are human beings and all whales have to do is be a whale and/or swim and/or eat whilst we as humans have considerably more to do on any given day, just take a look at my In Box. No. It's nothing to do with that difference at all.

We are talking about language here – pretty much the only thing we have (try taking any action without it being formulated and then captured in language).

And right now I'm going to use another form of language – written English – to point to where I'm going with this. So I'm going to write the sentence again with some punctuation:

WHALES DO NOT HAVE 'TOO MUCH TO DO'

That is the key phrase - 'too much to do' - as in:

'How are you doing?'

'Oh, OK thanks, but I've got too much to do'

Or its sister phrases, such as:

'I'm really busy'

or

'Actually, I'm a bit overwhelmed!'

Bentley and Chumley do not have too much to do!

My two St Bernard dogs are like whales. And the reason that

BENTLEY AND CHUMLEY DO NOT HAVE TOO MUCH TO DO

is once again NOT because they are dogs and we are human beings and all dogs have to do is be a dog and/or bark and/or eat whilst we as humans have considerably more to do on any given day, just take a look at my In Box. No.

No.

It's because Bentley and Chumley do not have language.

They are sitting right behind me as I write this and I have asked them. They don't.

My dogs can't think 'I have too much to do' and they can't say 'I have too much to do', so 'too much to do' doesn't show up in their life. Bentley and Chumley NEVER have 'too much to do' showing up in their lives.

And the reason you have 'too much to do' is because you do think and say it. And so it does show up for you. Consistently. Every day.

Just like everything else in your life. Everything shows up in your life as a function of how you language it.

'Too much to do' doesn't exist out there. It ONLY exists in here (David points to his head). And in our speaking.

And the first, critical step in addressing your sense of overwhelm is to simply delete language like that in your life. Cut it out. Stop it.

Stop it. Tell the truth instead

I've given up on the word 'busy' – try me, it doesn't pass my lips any more.

Why have I done that?

One of the reasons is because I realized that most of the time when I was saying the word, it was a lie. Not a lie because I had nothing to do. Not at all. Just like you, in my life there's always 'a list of things to do and be done and some come unexpectedly and all have varying degrees of urgency and importance accompanying them'.

So I have lots to do and so do you. Let's not get into a contest here about whose list of things to do is the longest. That's really not the point.

The reason it was a lie was because most of the time I didn't mean 'I'm busy' but (especially to my clients):

'I'm feeling really needy right now so I need you to know that just because I don't work in a Big Organization I don't sit around twiddling my thumbs all day'

or (especially to other consultants):

'I see you as a competitor in a Universe of scarce clients and so I need you to know that my business is successful'

or, unfortunately, often I really meant (to lots of people):

'I may indeed have just said Yes to your request but I'll probably let you down and not deliver on time and in full and I hope the code word 'busy' we've just used will encourage you to be complicit with me in forgiving me for letting you down…'

Or more positively, sometimes when I said 'I'm busy' I actually meant:

'I'm not at all 'busy'. My life is full of amazing things I get to do, things that are in my circle of influence because of the sort of work I do and how I've chosen to lead my life. I'm not 'busy'. I'm abundant in things to do! I love that these are mine to do!! How lucky am I?!'

But I used to chicken out and say 'I'm busy' instead. Everyone else was saying it, and I wanted to be cool like them, and fit in.

But not any more.

Complete your own personal translations of the word 'busy'. Be curious about what's going on for you when you want to say 'I'm busy'. And experiment with telling the truth instead.

You never have too many emails

You can give me – as in you can 'put into my hands' - a laptop or you can give me a phone or you can even give me a kiss. All these things have dimension, mass, texture, they take up physical space – but you can't give me 'too much to do'.

'Too much to do' only exists as a chunk of language, a thought form manifested in words.

'Ah' you say, 'But here's my inbox in that very same laptop I've given you and you can see it has 100 unread emails in it and I know that at least 60 of those have to be responded to by 8pm and there's only one hour to go to that deadline – THAT's too much to do!!'

The only reason this list of things means 'you have too much to do' is because you and I agree that this is what it is going to mean.

And given that I can see the emotional reaction your 'busy' meaning generates in you (I notice it rarely makes you happy to say 'I'm busy')

- and also because some of that anxiety is beginning to transfer to me (because we are all, after all, energetic beings) causing me to be stressed too -

I have decided to stop sharing that meaning with you. If you want to be 'busy' that's your thing not mine.

We have a choice.

Let's slow down and look at this.

You have 650 unread emails with a deadline coming soon.

You can indeed label that reality with the words 'busy' or 'too much to do'. After all it seems inevitable to do that. Everyone is using those terms.

But let's be clear that the words have an impact, on you and others. It's the label that produces anxiety. It's NOT the 650 emails, but the label we use. And then the feeling infects the thinking, so we get into victim mode with thoughts like

There shouldn't be 650 emails

I'm drowning here

If I were in charge of this place there would be a better process but I am not

There must be something wrong with me to get so far behind

and all those thoughts stimulate the anxiety and so on. It's a system. A closed loop.

So when you say you have 'too much to do' you think you are merely describing reality, and you think that you are reporting the reality that is causing your stress.

And I say that in fact it is exactly the opposite. Your instinct - personally and socially conditioned - to use that language is the cause of your stress.

Do this. That's all

Here's an alternative view.

We can all of us look back at our lives and see that the only thing we have ever done is what we did.

Slow down. Breathe that in!

There are never in fact '650 emails to be doing' (unless of course you really want that language and its consequent emotional drama in your life: hey, no one is forcing you to be free here).

No. There's only ever the one email to be doing. This one. I am doing this email. Now it is done. Here is the next email. Here I am doing it. Fully present to this email. Giving the task, the relationship, the words I type, my full attention.

I'm not distracted by the thought-form 'still 648 more to go though!' (that's never in fact as useful to me as it claims to be in my mind - what are we trying to do, motivate ourselves!?)

Here I am just doing the only thing I can do which is the thing I am doing right now. Nothing hanging over my head. Not dragging the weight of undone things around with me. Nothing heavy here.

Stress not 'managed': just never created.

I don't want to be left managing my stress. I want to get in at the start, and stop stress being made. And that starts with my words.

One email.

Words and the world, which came first?

So there's a distinction here.

First is the distinction of the 'Word to World Fit'. This is the distinction the majority of us are conditioned into.

It says this. There is a world out there, and we have learned certain labels to describe that world. This is a thing and I call it a tree. This is a thing and I call it a car. This is a list of emails to respond to and that means 'I'm busy'.

There is both personal and – probably even stronger – social pressure to ensure we continue to fit the right word to the right 'thing'. So we obediently say tree, car and busy.

Plus there's the payoff we get when it comes to the word 'busy' in particular as used in today's environment. The sympathy. The admiration. The complicity.

But I want to live a life more deliberate, more intentional than that.

I have something to say about how this thing called 'my experience' shows up for me. I don't want The sympathy. The admiration. The complicity. If I ever do, you'll hear me ask for them.

And I certainly don't want the stress. So I hope you'll never hear me ask for that, unless I am at my neediest.

And because I have decided that I have something to say about how my life shows up for me, I have decided to start with my language. I have decided to care A LOT about what comes out of my mouth.

Which is why I don't use the word 'busy' any more.

The second distinction is called 'World to Word Fit'

In other words, I cause to have the world

- this thing I call 'my experience' -

match my word, as much as I possibly can.

This is the realm of integrity.

For example, I say I will be on a call with you at 4pm on Tuesday and I am there. In other words, the world shows up as I said it would.

You ask me to complete the report by Friday at Noon, and I say Yes, and then I deliver it, on time and in full. Again, the world shows up as I said it would.

I have chosen peace. Not 'too much to do' Just the 'things I am choosing to do in the way I choose to be whilst doing them'

I have something to say about how the world occurs for me. And I have something to say about how I show up, as one of the things showing up in the world.

And so do you.

Bentley and Chumley do not have too much to do. And neither do you.

Watch 'me' change!

I read a book called *Constructive Living* by the psychotherapist David K Reynolds.

In it he recounts an experiment he was part of. He and a colleague

'received a grant from the National institute of Mental Health to create a depressed, suicidal person and send that researcher/patient into various psychiatric facilities in order to experience them from the inside'

(the goal, just in case it is not clear, was to deepen their understanding of how to treat depression effectively - not to show they could trick a hospital, like some reporter smuggling a knife past the TSA).

So the person they created for this experiment was David Kent – the surname being the middle name of the psychiatrist David K Reynolds, 'So David Kent' the author points out with no irony, 'is a part of me'.

For the experiment to succeed, first Reynolds had to learn how to become a suicidal depressive called David Kent. In short this proves the alchemical power of performance. As all actors know, the first way to get 'into character' is to begin to move like you think the character would move. So Reynolds spent hour after hour slowing right down, sitting with slumped shoulders, breathing shallowly. He only then had to start repeating depressive words to himself – talking to himself about how depressed he was - and soon enough the feelings followed. He became, over time and with intention, depressed.

But what was created in this experiment was more than just personal feelings, a private experience. As Reynolds recounts, scientific test after scientific test measured Kent to be truly depressed, and so the hospital records were adjusted accordingly. Now the world shifted to reflect his performance. But there was no deceit here, not any more. Reynolds-as-Kent, he says, felt 'truly awful'.

In other words, he became who he had chosen to be. Who he had said he was.

And then the external world validated his choices, and not just in the hospital records. For those of us concerned by what information 'they' out there store about us because of our internet footprint and the like, there's a further challenge.

In the book's spookiest moment, 'Reynolds as Kent' describes being treated by one of his ex-students. Someone who had sat in lectures on the subject of depression delivered in medical school by Professor Reynolds was now treating 'Kent' in the mental wards and was unable to distinguish that in fact the two personalities were held in the same physical body. She literally didn't recognize him. There was no Reynolds. Only this depressed patient called Kent.

There are two simple but powerful lessons here:

1. We get to be who we decide and declare ourselves to be.

- so get clear: who do you intend being? Who do you say you are? What words do you use to describe yourself?

and

2. We only see what we are conditioned to see.

- so keep checking: what are your blind spots? What are your habitual ways of seeing others? OR How does the world keep seeing you in a way that does not allow you to be who you want to be?

As they used to say near the beginning of every episode of the US cop show 'Hill Street Blues': 'Let's be careful out there!'

Let's be intentional in our language.

Ready to be a poet?

Poetry, n, from *poiein 'create.'*

We are all poets, all performers, if we have something to share that we intend will make a difference. But here's a thing about difference-making:

Difference from Latin *de-* and *fere*, literally meaning 'to carry away'

Which serves to remind us that making a difference takes an effort, an intention, an effort of carrying.

That's more effort than many people are willing to make.

The effort involves realizing that there is a fire that burns in us. Something unique to each of us that deserves to be expressed.

Being willing to search for that inner truth is not the work of the world: it's a very private and special and personal assertion of identity.

It sets us aside from the tribe when we undertake that work.

Poetry is not an expression of the party line. It's that time of night, lying in bed, thinking what you really think, making the private world public, that's what the poet does.
Allen Ginsberg, *Ginsberg: A Biography*
Barry Miles (1989).

We all get to be born. That's the easy part. Being born is not the poetry.

What we can also get is to find out who we really are. Who we intend *being* having been born. And to say that. That's where the poetry – the creating – comes to life. Speaking *you* – not as a polished script, not like some closing statements from the lawyer in court – but as an ongoing process. The poem you are gets spoken in your work, in your relationships, in your triumphs and insights and your endurance in the face of challenge, and it never ends:

I have never started a poem yet whose end I knew. Writing a poem is discovering.
Robert Graves

So is your life: discovering…

Up To Something

I know what you *think*. You keep telling me.

But I want to know what you are up to.

I want to know what you are committed to.

Please put it in words for me.

Tell me: what's your *gage*?

Engagement: they have it all wrong

Engagement: from French *engager* 'to pledge'

Or OF *gage*: To stake, pledge or wager

Back in Medieval times, when you gave someone a *gage*, you had just made a promise, and all of a sudden you had some skin in the game.

'Thank you for the loan of your field for my flock of sheep, Gerald of Kayleigh; my *gage* is that if I do not have the sheep out of your field by next summer's end, as I promise I will, then you can have one of my oxen in return.'

As I say, skin in the game.

Indeed, if you have movie memories of knights in armor challenging other knights in armor to a duel by slapping them on the cheek with a laced white glove, you'll be remembering another historical use of *gage*:

- a glove or other object thrown down to indicate a challenge to combat

(also as in the phrase we still use: *throwing down the gauntlet*)

And this of course was real skin in the game, since the subsequent duel was likely to be to the death. A *gage* is not something like its symbol – all flowery and lacey glove: your *gage* is your commitment to make a stand for what you believe to be right. You would lay down your life when you gave your *gage*.

But that's all in the past. Engagement now is a weak word, almost always coupled with the word Employee. Organizations worldwide invest billions of dollars to raise the engagement of their staff, seeking to have people be fully invested in their work, such that they'll perform better for the company.

It's a noble intention, but it's all the wrong way round. I don't want to work for a company, hoping they'll do nice things to make me more engaged so that then I'll switch on my performance engine. I want to make a *gage*:

'Thank you for that salary you put into my bank account every month. I appreciate it. I get to do nice things with it. While you continue to do that, by the way, my promise is that you'll get everything it says in my job description from me and more. Not because you please me or even care about me. But because I have made a *gage*. A promise. And I want to live my life in alignment with the promises I make.'

Engagement is not a matter of satisfaction, emotional attachment or even meaning.

Engagement is a matter of integrity.

'How engaged am I?' is not something you should ask in the context of what your employer is doing or not doing, and what you'd hope they'd do.

'How engaged am I?' is a question you should ask about your life.

What's the promise you made to yourself about who you wanted to be in the world? And how are you doing against that promise?

What a performance!

Back in 1990, my theater partner and I left the world of the stage and set up a training company, transferring the skills of acting to helping people do better business presentations ("Leigh Firth Associates: Performing for Business" it said on our business cards).

It was our mentor Peter Sole who set us on our way, concerned as he no doubt was about two actors being even more out of work now they'd given up on their theater company. It was Peter who told us that there were such things as presentations and that our experience might be transferable to helping people develop their skills and confidence when they had to do those presentations.

So we went to buy all the books on 'presentation skills' that we could find so that we could adapt our theater-based understandings to the language of business.

And we called our workshop *The Performance Program*, because we wanted to set ourselves apart from the marketplace by not using the word *presentation*. And because we wanted to assure our participants that although we'd be getting them to roll around on the floor like gorillas, we were truly interested in *performance* as in 'generating business results'.

It was only later that I realized the true power of the word Performance in this context.

Performance is from the Anglo-Norman *perfourmer* meaning to furnish, to manifest, literally 'to give form to'.

When actors perform they give form to what is invisible to the audience: the words and ideas of the playwright.

> Think when we talk of horses, that you see them
> Printing their proud hoofs i' the receiving earth;
> For 'tis your thoughts that now must deck our kings,
> Carry them here and there; jumping o'er times,
> Turning the accomplishment of many years
> Into an hour-glass...
> W Shakespeare, *Henry V*, Prologue

In EXACTLY the same way, when a business person does a presentation, they are not simply presenting information, they are giving form to – making manifest and real – the invisible, whether that is the strategy, the project or the sales targets for next year.

None of those things exist unless given form in the speaking of them.

Honestly, they really don't. Walk down the corridor and you cannot trip over next year's sales targets. Next years sales targets only exist as understandings reinforced and expressed through words.

All of us, in business or out of it, are performers.

The words we use will make a reality real and tangible. How intentional are yours?

You're nervous because you have nothing to say!

People came on our course wanting to 'get over their nerves' or 'conquer their fear of audiences'.

The assumption here was that the source of the fear was out there in 'reality.'

'Because there is a group of people looking at me, I get nerves. And I don't like that feeling…'

- this, by the way, a bad feeling, experienced in the body, *caused purely linguistically*: the label 'nerves' - or 'abject terror' - are simply words chosen by the participant as apparently accurate representations of what is in fact a purely physiological/chemical phenomenon: actors back stage about to walk on stage are exhilarated – *come alive!* – when they experience the same bodily phenomenon: they don't say 'Oh God, nerves'; they say 'This is what I was born to do!' -

'…so please give me a technique for getting over my nerves'.

I've since worked out what was really missing from my participants: they didn't have anything to say.

That was the void they were trying to fill with 'tips' and 'techniques' for 'looking confident'.

But they didn't have anything to say. That's why the 'tips' and 'techniques' only helped a little, or a lot but temporarily.

Yes, I grant you, they had stuff that they were supposed to communicate. They had strategies, and projects and the sales targets for next year. But their deepest sense of self was beginning to realize that this was not what their life was about.

Now, please understand, it can be: if you truly OWN the sales targets for next year as your Henry V – and there's no reason you can't or shouldn't – then you won't have nerves.

But most of the people I worked with – still work with – experience a gap between what they 'have to' say and what they truly would want to stand in front of a group and declare.

Give me a person with something to say

Give me a person with something they truly want to say and nerves don't enter into it. Will they say it as gloriously as Martin Luther King? Maybe not. Will they stumble and stammer? Perhaps. Will they experience a physiological adrenaline rush, which they can they label whatever they choose. Sure.

The only difference is that nerves now won't be the show stopper.

What do you want to say?

Start with that question.

Not 'What do you want to be?' or 'What do you want to do?'

Just 'What do you truly want to say to make a difference in the world?'

Do you have anything to say to the world?

The forms of things unknown, the poet's pen
Turns them to shapes, and gives to airy nothing
A local habitation and a name.
W Shakespeare, *A Midsummer Night's Dream*

Speaking up is risky

The cavemen sit around the fire together. It feels good. It feels safe. All the dangers of the world are outside the cave.

And then someone from the circle stands and says 'I have something to say'.

At the moment they leave the safety of the group.

But someone has to.

If you want to change your world, your words will take a risk – they'll risk your identity, they'll risk your friend's safe identity, they'll shake up your team, they'll threaten the status quo.

If you don't want to change your world, keep your words safe, keep your true voice – the voice of your heart – to yourself. Keep saying only what the tribe expects you to say.

Voice vox L. communicate, articulate, declare, state, assert, reveal, proclaim, announce, publish, publicize, make public, make known, table, air, vent; utter, say, speak.

Speak up.

Speak out.

Speak.

How I gave my work a voice

My first two years out of theater and in the business world were some of the most miserable years of my life. Why? Because Alan and I were desperate to be accepted by 'business people' – we thought they were a different form of human being than us. We thought we needed to show how knowledgeable and smart we were about business. We thought we – with our six years of causing audiences around the world to laugh and cry, to imagine things that weren't really there – were not enough.

One of the ways we dealt with this existential anxiety about our self-worth was by eliminating risk. So we scripted our workshops, line by line, moment by moment, such that we could never put a foot wrong (because we believed business people respected certainty). We played our workshops not to lose.

And what I found was that all the passion and playfulness and creativity and improvisation – the stuff that caused our theater work to be so successful and vital – drained out of our workshops.

I was as a trainer 'mouthing a script' in a dead way that I'd never done, even when all the words I uttered on stage were originally created by Shakespeare or Swift or Rabelais.

Strange.

I learnt that words are life and death.

Your voice is your heart

Eventually, I decided to throw away the script and replaced it with what I truly wanted to share. About performance. About danger. About risk. About exposing yourself. About daring to talk. About speaking from the heart as opposed to what you thought the audience wanted to hear.

In those first two years I was 'acting' – simply showing up and saying the right words in the right way – in a way I never had in the theater. It was dead. It was robotic. It was lifeless.

So I gave up wanting to sound good.

And when I learnt to trust myself, to connect with what mattered, with what I wanted to share – and spoke to that – then the workshops came to life. And I began to make a real difference in people's lives:

I just wanted to mail you to say thanks. I can honestly say that without you I could not have gone through with it [giving a presentation at a major conference]. *You made me believe in myself and my ability to get up there and do this and for that I am eternally grateful. Your course was excellent and I would recommend it to anyone. Thanks again David, you were an inspiration and a brilliant mentor.*

Authenticity is authordom

Author: c.1300, autor "father," from O.Fr. auctor, from L. auctorem (nom. auctor) "enlarger, founder, master, leader," lit. "one who causes to grow," agent noun from auctus, pp. of augere "to increase"

When people start to live their lives from what matters to them most of all, from what is most true to them; when they learn to speak that truth from the heart as opposed to saying what they think will make them look good, they call that 'being authentic'.

They are correct. They get to be at the start of things, the cause of what they want to create, like an author is the cause of the book we then read.

They get to start at Chapter One. And they realize they have a say in how all the other Chapters are going to develop. And grow. And increase the world.

What is this 'real world' you love so much?

As in:

'Ah yes, David, but we have to live in the real world, don't we?'

or

'I'm just being realistic!'

This is what I call the 'conversational trump card'. The assertion that whatever we might have just been discussing – however exciting or intriguing or moving it might have been for you – is now about to dissolve in the face of

REALITY

As if

REALITY

is anything other than a concept described and negotiated in language.

'An angry dog'.

'A juicy steak'.

'A beautiful sunrise'.

'Reality'.

All just words awaiting an agreement.

And I've noticed that 100% of the time, the

    REALITY

    that you argue for is always a meaner, scarier, less attractive place than the future you'd only minutes ago been contemplating creating.

    I don't know why you would choose that.

    There's the Bigger Life we know we could be addressing.

    Then there's the Smaller Life of contingencies and bargaining which we convince ourselves is necessary and practical and 'real'.

    But its reality is in fact dependent on others playing at that level with us.

    I won't.

    Will you?

So many words a day

If, as research carried out by the University of Arizona suggests

…women in the study spoke a daily average of 16,215 words during their waking hours, versus an average of 15,669 words for men
http://www.sciencedaily.com/releases/2007/07/07070515 2953.htm

- which means we will speak *370 million words* in an average lifetime -

how many of those words actually make a difference?

How many of those words will:

>Encourage
>Empower
>Embolden
>Grow
>Declare commitment or make a promise
>Apologize and mend?

As opposed to how many of those millions of words will:

>Justify
>Explain
>Reinforce our position

Make us feel good
Defend
Attack?

Let's go on a word diet.

Your words change your economy!

My new balance sheet:

Commitments, promises,
requests made today = PROFITS

Blah, blah, blah = WASTAGE, WRITE-OFFS

Words that change your world

I talk with people about the power of promises to alter reality.

Hear that. Not 'promise' as in 'good intention' or 'I hope'.

The power of promises to alter reality.

When you make a promise, you shift the reality that is now going to happen.

I use the example of wedding vows to illustrate this in a way that most people in my audiences get. They're either already married, or they used to be married, or they are considering the possibility that they might one day be married.

Wedding ceremonies differ from culture to culture, religion to religion, secular society to secular society, but whatever their distinctive characteristics, I haven't come across a single wedding ceremony that does not have at the heart of it a conversation

A conversation.

A conversation wherein two people make promises to each other.

And unless the two people make those promises, there is no marriage.

Before the words, no marriage. After the words, a different world.

The marriage is not created by the priest or the officer or the chapel or the flowers or the guests in attendance.

The marriage exists *because* the promises were made.

(In my culture: "I now declare you man and wife" – that declaration itself being a creative act)

Words stronger than life itself

I then ask people who have been married what state they were in when that conversation unfolded.

Not the giddiness of waking that morning in anticipation. Not the happy party afterwards, But the moments when that conversation of promise-making was initiated.

And even though we agree that we all knew exactly what words we were supposed to utter, that we had plenty of notice of what we were supposed to say, when the moment came actually for making the vows, our state lifts!

The voice trembles

The breathing shortens

The focus is Here and Now

We are alive!

(and every witness can sense that).

And why?

Because Promising is an elevated form of speaking.

It brings us back in touch with the power of our creating.

We are about to create something in our speaking.

'Do you…?'

No - because that's still an option! - ?

Or YES.

We can lift our words up

What if our life had more of that quality of speaking?

Not just once in a lifetime, but every day…

Sometimes people say to me, 'ah yes, David, but marriages don't always last. Promises get unmade'.

Yes they do. Median duration of first marriages that end in divorce:

Males: 7.8 years
Females: 7.9 years.

But I say there are people in your world who will make a promise tomorrow that they'll be breaking by lunchtime the same day.

That's not a promise.

That's just weak words made up to sound like a promise.

My friend Todd asks his clients, when they say they are committed to a course of action:

'Could your commitment run me over, like my truck?'

That's a solid promise!

I don't want to say 'I promise' when I really mean 'I'll try' or 'I hope to' or 'As long as nothing better comes up'.

I want to speak my Promises with Blood and Guts!

Let's have more Promises in our lives of a 7.85 year duration.

When words get in the way

When you have made your promise, check to see how it makes you feel.

Words should always empower you.

When they do the opposite, delete them.

Why would I do anything, why would I think any thought, why would I say any word

if it was going to make me fearful...?

It's that simple.

It's part of a word diet.

When my words spin out of control

Michael Neill and his mentor George Pransky do some great work on the nature of Mind and the inside out nature of experience.

I love their metaphor of 'thoughts spinning out of control' – I love it because it describes so well my own experiences of getting into crazy loops of stressed out worries and negative thoughts. It's like the thoughts are feeding on and building on each other, seemingly out of my conscious control, getting faster and faster, *spinning*, there's no other word for it, like a child's top. Or like a fan.

Michael writes:

++++++

Imagine the following scenario:

You are standing in front of a large electric fan, spinning at full speed. Your challenge is to to get a full deck of 52 playing cards through the blades of the fan to the other side. For each card you get through unscathed, you will receive $1000; each card that gets through damaged will earn you $250; each card that fails to get through will cost you $500.
What's the winning strategy?

While there are any number of fun things you might try, from flicking the cards one at a time to bundling them up tightly and attempting to get the whole pack through in one go, the simplest and most effective strategy is to unplug the fan and allow the blades to stop (or at least slow) before attempting to pass the cards through.

++++++

Don't try to 'fix' the thinking, then, is Michael's advice. Slow down. Breathe. Wait it out...*Then* move...

I've noticed my talking gets like that fan too.

Here I am, on the phone to my coach. And I'm talking. And talking. I'm telling him about the problem I'm facing. The problem is that over the course of the last three weeks, four clients have indicated that business I had considered to be booked and solid for later in the year is now not as definite as we'd agreed.

That's the problem in a nutshell. 39 words in fact. But that's not enough for me, because my fan has begun to spin. So I'm not just telling my coach about the problem, I'm telling him why the problem I'm facing is as it is. And then a bit more about how it's making me feel.

It's not that the words are wrong. On the contrary. The words are accurate. And I'm an articulate guy. I can talk. I can say things. I can choose the right word for maximum descriptive impact. I can, when needed, call a spade a spade, but I also know it can be called a cultivation implement.

So it's not that the words I am using are not doing a good job of describing my problem. I do notice that there's a lot of them though, as if telling Stephen a few more words, and then a few more, and a few more after that, will have him eventually say:

'Ah, NOW I get it, David. The world is indeed cruel and unjust! I thought you were just blathering on about your problems. But now, because you shared a few more words, I have been given access to a moment of illumination about the nature of this devious and unreliable universe. Thank you David!'

And it's not even that saying fewer words would be 'better'. It's rather that description is not what is required.

I've got to turn off the fan. I've got to stop using language as a describer, justifier, and enroller of others into my stories....

...and I've got to start using language to get me into action.

This involves two very simple (and notice: how succinct) questions, which Stephen, who never plugged his own fan in, asks me:

   a. What do I want? (easy: more revenue to replace the unsure revenue!)

   b. What am I prepared to do to have that happen? (easy: make a plan for generating business, implement the plan, repeat)

Description is nice, and necessary to a point, but I want to use my language like a warrior uses a sword. Cut through, cut down, cut to the chase...And questions are a powerful example of that way of using talk to create action.

Funnily enough, a few hours after closing my call with Stephen, I had a text message pop up on my phone from the network carrier:

'You have exceeded $100 in voice usage charges. You might want to manage your account online to avoid a costly bill.'

Thanks AT&T: I get it...

Turning the world upside down

I want to suggest:

>   The reader creates the writing

>   The audience creates the performance

>   The followers create the leader

>   The listening creates the connection

>   The Fool is the most powerful person in the King's Court

>   Words create your thoughts

>   Words create your actions

>   Try it on...

I can't move myself forward

Those of you with any working knowledge of Monty Python may remember a relatively minor sketch called 'Bruces' about a bizarre Australian 'university' where everyone was called Bruce ('to keep it simple!').

That sketch was inspired by an Australian Professor, Bruce 'G'day!' Mitchell, a world-renowned Medieval scholar (and I mean really, really academic: he died recently and his last essay as far as I know was about the use of the comma in 'Beowulf').

Bruce was my tutor at St Edmund Hall Oxford (Terry Jones from Monty Python went there too which is why this story is fitting together, honestly).

So Bruce Mitchell taught me Old English, which has been almost totally useless to me other than one not-useless thing at all: the amazing love it has left for me for language and how it works, and a fascination with words and where they come from.

And the word 'afford' comes from OE ge-forthian, a verb meaning to advance, to further, to move forward or promote.

So when someone says to me

'I can't afford you'

or they say to themselves:

'I can't afford the time'

I've realized that they are saying 'I can't advance myself' or 'I can't further myself right now'.

It's not that they can't afford me – or the time - it's that they can't 'afford' themselves.

Because as a coach and consultant, I have worked out, I'm not selling *me*. I'm selling the 'advanced' them...

Words that make life work out

My new mantra:

> Work Out What You Really Want
>
> Declare It, Using Your Most Blood And Guts Words
>
> Do Your Best To Create That
>
> Then See What Happens

That's all there is...

We ask for things with words

Our lives are as they are because we have had the conversations we've had, and because we've said the things we've said. We've made requests, promises, exhortations, apologies, justifications, demands, predictions and told stories – and in this way we've talked our world into being.

She has that house now because she asked for that promotion back then.

He has that career now because he asked for the brochure from the training college back then.

You have that marriage, good, bad or indifferent, because you made or responded to a request – *will you marry me?* – and then a vow – *I do*.

That man is lying dead and his neighbor is in a jail cell awaiting trial for murder because the two of them only ever had the conversation about how much one was right and the other was wrong about the tall hedge that bordered both their gardens.

Our world is created by 'conversational acts' – speaking and ways of speaking that bring forth a world that would not be there had we not spoken in that way.

Writes Vera in her online diary (*http://verabug.com/2004/01/11/*):

+++++

I just went through some of my old work emails

from my last job.

I found in the Drafts folder:

This message has not been sent.

Subject: raise

Hi Charlie,

:::::::::

I am such a chicken!

++++

Vera has worked out that raises happen in language.

Asking creates an outcome: whether it's the one we intended or not, at least we know it and can then work with it.

Not asking creates a chicken.

We might get what we ask for. We certainly don't get what we don't ask for…

Burned out by saying burned out

As I was writing this afternoon, I had a call from an associate who asked me to coach a client of hers.

Apart from his geographical location – near to me, hence the call – the first thing she said about the client was that he was 'burned out'.

I wonder if he labeled himself the same way? Because if he did then that was the source of his problems, and not the articulation of them.

Just like breathing. Words so easily said, but always with such huge consequence…

Change the word, change the behavior

I have a friend who has made some breakthroughs recently around his habit of 'people pleasing'. Increasingly he has been able to notice when he's doing it, and where he's coming from when he is doing it. This is a great shift for him. I remember that when we first identified this habit as something he might want to look at, he was pretty defensive.

'What could be so wrong with other people liking me?'

There's nothing wrong with that, of course. It's when we make it our goal that people like us, or our drive, or our reason for being, that things can get a bit strange.

Ultimately we find ourselves in danger of constructing relationships based on what we can get from other people rather than what we can give to or serve them with.

Good work versus buttering up

As children we are taught to seek approval. Learning 'good behavior', for example, is based on other people being pleased with us and giving us a reward to reinforce what we did. My 8 year old son recently got to sit at his teacher's desk all day as a reward for good work. One of the things we learn early on in transactions like this is that saying the right thing produces a positive response in the teacher. And this is fine when 'saying the right thing' is at the level of giving the correct answer to the math question. But not as adults.

My son's teacher's reward system has some further lessons for us all. Everyone who completes all of the previous week's homework and assignments to a good standard gets to put a chip with their name on it into a black cloth bag. Several times during the week, the teacher pulls a name from the bag and that lucky student gets to come forward and draw from a second bag which has in it another set of chips with prizes written on them. The prizes range from great ones to small ones to some chips which have no prize at all. I like this. I think it teaches a very adult lesson. Good work might bring you a range of rewards – and, sometimes, not the rewards you were hoping for at all. But without the good work, you wouldn't even be in the bag.

So the lesson: do good work.

Pleasing is all wrong

We threaten the life we could lead when we are still trying to provoke positive responses in others as adults and are willing to 'say the right thing' even when what we say is not in alignment with our values or boundaries or authenticity.

The question really needs to be 'What is best for the other person to hear in the service of creating something better with them than their 'being pleased'?

There's a number of problems with people-pleasing or trying to get others to like us:

1. It's creepy

2. It's a form of self-harm – when we silence our own truth we are metaphorically strangling ourselves

3. It reduces them – as if we know that what they need above all else is to think good things of us

4. It's based on a lie – we tell ourselves pleasing people is good for them when in fact it's always done for us. The opposite of pleasing people is serving them; the former is selfish, the latter is self-less

5. It's playing small – there is courage required in saying what needs to be said rather than withholding or manipulating in order to have someone like you.

6. The results are in fact unpredictable because people can be inconsistent. They may like you right now, but not at this time tomorrow.

7. There isn't necessarily a correlation between someone being pleased with you and that someone giving you what you believe you deserve.

This last one is particularly true in the corporate world. We have a story that promotion is given on merit - and a lot of the time it is and a lot of the time it isn't. Who gets what next job is often driven by politics, favor-trading and unexamined perceptions and stories on the part of the decision-makers (and then, afterwards, our own unexamined perceptions and stories about the decision-makers, which are often just as destructive to healthy functioning).

Stop using the words need and deserve

Here's a question:

What if we lived our lives as if no-one has anything we need to get from them?

We may still in fact get what they have power to give us, but the value of our life, and our happiness and self-worth, is not built on whether we get it or not. The chips are ALWAYS going to fall where they may and we need to be big enough to respond healthily to any outcome.

And what if we lived our lives without ever using the words 'I deserve...' as in 'I deserve that promotion!' Or at least not in the sense of 'deserve' we have now.

Deserve vb 1250–1300; Middle English deserven < Anglo-French, Old French deservir, Latin dēservīre *to devote oneself to the service of, to serve well or zealously*

Let's get the entitlement out of 'I deserve' and get back to zealous service!

The word *please*, incidentally, comes from L. placare which as well as the meaning we now have, also has the sense of *to soothe, quiet*, as in the modern word placate. Soothing and quieting is what I want to do with my baby, but I don't want to do it with my life. I don't want a quiet, soothed life, I want my life to be loud and edgy

> *If you're not living on the edge, you're taking up too much room*
> Anon

You can declare who you are

Many people never become who they could have been because they never put it into words.

I say don't waste that opportunity.

We get to live our lives as we say we will live it. We set our own standards, our own vision for a great life (with great work as a substantial part of that). We declare our own commitment to This Is Who I Am. And we make that commitment big and juicy and scary so that it stretches us and pulls us forward and we can look at it and know that if we truly live our life like that, then we'll be spent by the end of it and with no danger of dying with our music still inside us.

> The biggest service you can give to the world is to be profoundly, expansively you.
>
> The biggest service you can give to the world is to be profoundly, expansively you.
>
> The biggest service you can give to the world is to be profoundly, expansively you.

Then, having declared This Is Who I Am, we get to experience how deeply rewarding it is to Be that person.

And the outcome, ironically, is that we still get the rewards – we get to sit at teacher's desk – and we get to have people who are pleased with us. But we are not being who we are being SO THAT we will get rewards, or

SO THAT people will like us. We've turned the relationship on its head.

And there's a resilience there that was not there in the world of hoping someone else will give us what we want. If we get the promotion we are happy, because we have been Who I Am. And if we don't get the promotion we are happy, because we have been Who I Am and will begin again tomorrow.

We don't get what we deserve; we get what we create. And that creation always includes who we are being, moment after moment, however the chips have fallen.

My friend found the missing piece

This Is Who I Am was the missing piece in my friend's leadership development plan. Development plans are strong on goals and targets and strategies to get us there. Plans like this are based on solid psychology. It is good to have direction in our lives. It is good to have goals that are motivating. And it is reassuring that we can create a strategy to give a sense of clarity to break down our dreams into projects.

But as they are, development plans like these make a huge assumption: they exist as if who we are is our results and achievements. But we are more than that. Just hang around to see what they talk about at your funeral. If the elegy they speak at your funeral sounds only like a final recital of your résumé, there'll probably only be dry eyes in the place.

This Is Who I Am is a powerful input into – actually, the ultimate driver – of *What I Intend to Achieve* and needs to be created and declared.

The curse for choosing words poorly

Language n. from L lingua *tongue*

I speak only English but meet many people who are multi-lingual: they have many tongues.

I am curious: do they hear what I say to them in English and translate those English words into, say, French ones before they think whatever they think about it? Is there a gap? Is it simultaneous? What's the reverse process?

For years as a teenager and college student I lived with a poster of Bruegel's painting *The Tower of Babel*

Then they said, "Come, let us build ourselves a city, with a tower that reaches to the heavens, so that we may make a name for ourselves..."
Genesis 11

God's curse for their presumption? Locusts? Boils? No. Worse than all that. Not being able to understand each other. It made their work so difficult they had to stop.

What do I hear my voice saying?

And is that the same as what 'I' want to say?

Leaving yourself speechless

I have a client who keeps telling me what's going to happen. Or rather he is telling me what isn't going to happen.

'There won't be any change in our leadership team, David, because the CEO won't force X and Y to change – and they are the ones who most need to change'.

'Have you told him that?'

'No'.

'Perhaps you could'.

'Why should I speak up when I know it won't make any difference?'

It's a self-reinforcing loop.

Fear. Playing small. Protecting myself *because*…

I could focus on the thinking aspects of my client's situation here, or his internal stance: the predicting of an inevitable future; the blame game; the victim mentality in claiming powerlessness. But for now I want to focus here on the speaking aspects.

There's so much being constrained here.

There's my client's voice, trapped inside him, unable to be heard, dead before birth.

There's what that voice might share – the riches it might bring to his team in terms of his perspective, his experience, his authenticity, his values in action.

And there's what his voice might shift in other people. Not that - if he speaks up about his concerns in the next team meeting – it need be a beautiful expression of rhetoric with exactly the right vocabulary or phrases; a masterpiece of oratory. It doesn't have to be that. That his voice is heard at all expressing his truth will be in itself a symbol for others that things might change, and maybe the very thing his colleagues need to hear to shift the whole team forward.

Our words matter. But it need not be in the content of what we say: just that we spoke up at all. That we stained the silence.

Do you really mean that you are frustrated?

I've heard business people use the word 'frustrated' to describe any emotion they are currently feeling, from

vaguely discontented

to

absolutely furious.

I'd invite you to have a look at what really might be going on for you when you say that word.

Frustration has become a weak word, the default, robotic word business (wo)men use – when asked 'How do you feel?' – to hide their real emotions, which are more likely to be at that moment closer to sheer terror or pitiless rage.

The last client I heard say 'I'm frustrated' really wanted to say 'What is going on around me is a significant challenge to the fundamental values I hold dear in my life; I feel compromised and taken advantage of'. After some coaching, he did get to say that out loud, because out loud – as opposed to rattling around inside his head – is a positive step towards change.

> Frustration mid-15c., from L. frustratus, pp. of frustrari "to deceive, disappoint, frustrate," from frustra (adv.) "in vain, in error," related to fraus "injury, harm."

The origin word *fraus* indicates that what might be going on when people say they are frustrated is some damage to their integrity or values.

Stop saying frustration.

Name the real emotion.

Ask

'How is my integrity being challenged by this situation,
and what can I do to take control?'

And then do that.

How to find the music in your organization

Many of the people I coach or consult to spend many of their waking hours inside some form of organization or other.

Their relationship to the organization is a word-based one. For too many of them, the word 'organization' has come to mean

A great unwieldy behemoth that doesn't care about us and gets in the way of what we're hoping to do. A machine. A maze of unreasonable laws and constraints. Something to be complained about. Something very, very difficult to change.

Interestingly, the word organization comes from

mid-15c noun of action from organizare, from L. organum "instrument, organ"

An organization is an instrument.

My father, bless him, was a Lay Reader in the Church of England Faith. One of the side effects of this was that I spent almost every Sunday of my childhood twice a week in church. The rituals, prayers and hymns of all those services are, as a result, still held in my memory, albeit now as fragments.

One of those fragments is a line from the famous prayer of St Francis of Assisi:

'Lord, make me an instrument of thy peace'

- instrument here as in L. organum.

So in the prayer there is something wanting to be manifested – in this case Peace – and I am asking to be an instrument for it, a channel for it, an organization for it. Because, the implication is, unless I am the right kind of instrument, Peace isn't going to exist in the world. There is no other way. I may want the world to be peaceful. But it isn't happening unless it starts with me.

So too we might stress less about our business organizations by seeing them not as barriers but as conduits for the reason the business exists at all. And each of us as an organization – an instrument of that Purpose – within it.

Any 'business re-organization' project needs to spend more time on re-connecting to the why of the business than it does playing about with structures.

And so too we need to ask ourselves how well we are channeling the essential purpose of the business. There's something bigger than any of us trying to be born.

Are we as individuals set up – in our moods, attitudes, skills, behaviors, or words – for that channel?

So too in my personal life, what's my purpose, my highest possibility, and are my thoughts, words and actions in alignment with that, so it can come through clearly and without friction?

Lord, make me an instrument of my purpose...

No action without the word

I will rescue 'reality' from the 'Action! Heroes,' those that have for centuries urged us:

'Just do it!'

or

'Enough of all this talking, let's take action!'

These sentences are some of the coolest things you could be heard to say in a business meeting, despite the fact that they are often spoken by people who haven't worked out that their many, many, many, many, many, many, many actions have got them into this mess in the first place.

Action? We love speaking about how great action is. It's so virile to speak like that!

But it's speaking based on confused thinking.

For most people who are looking for action – or 'the right behavior' – they see action as Our Savior. The thing that is going to make all the difference. The colussus striding over the world that will take us from here to there.

That action is the thing that manifests intention into results is not up for debate here. My point is that it is *already always doing that* anyway.

In the triumverate *Think, Say, Do* at the heart of all my work, Do is not distinct from the other two as in '*and then* we must act to make it happen'.

There's never an *'and then'*.

Your thoughts and talking (to self and others) have already inevitably produced a result. Even 'nothing happened' is a result! And where did 'nothing happened' come from? From the same place results always come from: from the nature and quality of your thinking and talking.

Weak, unchallenged or unintentional thinking and talking produces weak results.

Stop listening to those macho guys who love to talk about 'Action!'. Action is no wolf, devouring reality into success. Action is a dog on the lead of Thoughts and Talking. Action is no Hero. Action is the whelp child of your thinking and talking.

Action doesn't drive anything, let alone change. On the contrary, it does exactly – quite literally – as it is told. You make action big by creating big, purposeful, assumption-challenged thoughts and making big, robust, intentional agreements with others through conversations with them.

Show me a powerful result in your company, or in your life, and I will show you a set of powerful agreements – words spoken – leading up to that result.

Show me a weak or unintended result and I will show you a thread of weak words and weak agreements, naturally and inevitably leading up to that result you say you don't want.

No more action is going to alter anything unless you get some powerful, intentional, blood and guts words in your life.

If action is happening in your life as you want it to then it's because the talking – the commitments, the promises, the agreements - have been sufficient.

If it is not happening, then they have not been. So you need more talk.

Action gets born in talking.

Let's resolve to simply create

Ever made a (New Year's) Resolution?

Did it have blood and guts to it?

Or did it sound like:

I'll try. But don't count on it.

And then we look back after a couple of months of the year and we can trace our poor results to the weakness of the resolution. We are like the Philip Larkin poem 'As Bad As A Mile'. Here is that poem in its entirety:

Watching the shied core
Striking the basket, skidding across the floor,
Shows less and less of luck, and more and more

Of failure spreading back up the arm
Earlier and earlier, the unraised hand calm,
The apple unbitten in the palm.

It's a cliché that New Year's Resolutions are as likely to fail – almost at the moment of their inception, like Larkin's disastrous apple – as they are to succeed.

As with promises, we should think carefully about doing them at all rather than devalue their currency by 'having another go'.

The weakness in most New Year's Resolutions comes from a subliminal confusing of *resolution* with *revolution* – at the revolving of the year we consider turning around our behavior, from this to that, from no gym to lots of gym, from lots of booze to no booze.

More power would come from replacing the *revolving* concept. It never feels like a true *volte face* in any case, I find, more like wrestling a recalcitrant mule to move when it doesn't want to. So let's replace *turning* with *creating*.

And at the source, the start, the *birth* of a new year, let's tap into all that sense of BEGINNING and create something new in our lives.

And here's where we can access the origins of the word *resolution*: the process of reducing things into simpler forms.

Resolution. Early 15c., "a breaking into parts," from L. resolutionem (nom. resolutio) "process of reducing things into simpler forms"

So let's strip our creating down into its essential elements.

First, let's not have it burdened with *trying* to or *hoping to* or *being motivated to*. Let's keep those weak words out of our mouths.

And what are the essential elements of human creation?

Think, Say, Do.

Nothing else.

So, for example, say I am resolved to create health and vitality in my life, and one of the channels for that will be the gym.

What's the highest, most productive <u>thought</u> I could have about this? That health and vitality is an adventure for me? Or an expression of what I could become in the world? Or the foundation of my integrity? Let's create that thought in words that speak to us, that resonate with our internal 'instrument'.

And what are the <u>conversations</u> I can have that will have that thought come about in my life? Regular Friday afternoon check-ins with my personal trainer about commitment to next week's gym times? Yes.

And <u>Do</u>? See the chapter about *Action*. Weak agreements, weak results: strong agreement, strong results…Lining up my life with my Integrity. I'll either be in the gym when I said I would, or I won't. If I'm not there, it wasn't a Promise.

Period.

Learning to bend with grace

This is a book about Change.

My work as a consultant and coach is about having people create change in their lives and companies.

Change starts with words – 'I promise…' or 'We are committed to…' - and Change is also stopped in words.

For many people, change is stopped with the word *change* itself.

Change.

Put fifty people in a room together and give them three minutes to brainstorm all that comes to mind for them when they think of 'change' and my experience of running exactly that exercise leads me to conclude that 80% of the words they use to describe change are negative.

Even when they remind themselves to be positive and say 'ah yes, and of course *change is the start of something new'* they sound like they'd rather be processing their last month's expenses receipts than creating something powerful.

Change has become a weasel word. It has come to mean:

A stress-inducing alteration from what makes one comfortable or safe; an imposition forced on us by people claiming to make things better but in fact making things worse; the unpredictability of the future; an unavoidable inevitability, but generally about as welcome as taxation.

In organizations, Managing Change has come to mean:

To seek control over what ought to happen; to determine how things turn out; to have to deal with people and their feelings and their resistance and such.

In politics also, change has become saturated with cynicism and second-guessing.

If ever a word needed re-empowering as a word of action, as a blood and guts word, it is *change*!

Let's have a look at the origins of the word

c.1225, from O.Fr. changier, from L.L. cambiare, from L. cambire "to exchange, barter," from PIE base *kamb- "to bend, crook."

These origins remind us of what we can often forget when faced with change: that all change is an *exchange*. Something may be taken away, but something is always given in return. It is important to discipline ourselves to locate both elements, and not focus only on the loss or the negative.

In this *exchange*, we can see too that there is something we are both giving and receiving in any change. What are we asked to take from the change that is coming? What are we being asked to give to it? These can be profound questions, but in exploring them we can find the personal growth that leads to better confidence, esteem and power for future changes.

And in the concept of 'Kamb', we can contemplate any change from the viewpoint of *bending to accommodate the change*. It causes us to consider that any reaction to change that causes us to go rigid – by being tough or hard in the mistaken idea that this is the same as 'being strong' – is not going to be the most productive response.

How can we bend ourselves to the change, like the branches of a tree in the wind?

The trunk of a tree is solid – as are our values or commitments – but the branches move – as may our mindset, emotions, attitude or behaviors.

'Kamb' is also the source of *camber* which, amongst other things, is the convex curvature of a road. Why is a road made like that? For two reasons: it helps cars stay gripped to the road, particularly around more severe bends, and because it helps the rainwater drain off. In both cases, having a camber is useful. Indeed it is suggested that one of the main historical examples of *kambing* was to bend a branch such that it could be turned into a bow for hunting. Again, kambing makes the branch more useful.

So here is another challenge: how can we encourage ourselves and each other to find the *usefulness* of the change we are being asked to consider? What is being made more useful – by development or improvement of the existing state – by embracing this change? And, finally, how can we be more useful to this change, rather than standing back and wishing it weren't happening?

The Future

future
late 14c., from O.Fr. futur, from L. futurus "about to be," irregular suppletive future participle of esse "to be."

The future is you about to be you. Who will that be?

Creating your future is your work in the world

When I came out of the theater world back in 1991, my partner and I set up a training company. It allowed us to play a role we had never played before: the role of 'business people' (maybe we were also playing the role of 'people who finally got a real job'!).

As business people, we bought the suits, we bought the desk (which we put in my partner's spare bedroom) and we did all sorts of other things we'd heard business people did like putting motivating posters up on the wall.

One of these posters we made for ourselves and it said 'What have you done for LFA today?' – LFA being our company name. We loved it. It kept us focused on getting stuff done, on contribution. And then one day our Business Mentor – actually my partner's wife's boss – said:

"You know what it should say underneath that, boys?"

"No" we said.

"It should say 'What have your done for LFA *tomorrow*?'"

He was right of course. Getting everything done today – even getting everything done really well – may not necessarily leave the company better off for tomorrow ('tomorrow' in this sense meaning either literally tomorrow; or next week; or next quarter; or four years from now). His advice spoke to the fact that we regularly need to think strategically and from the bigger picture so that the longer term health of the business isn't sacrificed at the altar of today's busy-ness.

If we work for a company or cause, our work, even though it may not be written in our job descriptions, is to operate with what Charles Handy calls 'a sense of continuity'. Charles Handy is a management writer and consultant who used to work for Shell, a company that is over one hundred years old. He says that he worked out early in his career working for Shell that although his job title may well have been 'Regional Economist', he was also expected to operate as a Guardian of Shell's Future, since it, as a company, had plans of being around a lot longer than him.

And whether we now work for a company or cause, or have retired from one, or are thinking about joining one, or are always going to independent of 'employment', we all need to give ourselves a chance to step out of our today and focus on our tomorrow. We are all Guardians of our own and the world's Future. We all need not just to do the work required today but also work to leave our lives better off for the future.

Ask:

What is the best version of my life I can imagine?

When I say that out loud, do my words have blood and guts to them?

Now what am I prepared to do to create that future?

Because your future creates your present

There was one more insight that our mentor was revealing to us, though I didn't get it until many years afterwards. It is this: that people's energy and attitude (and with that their performance) is ignited not from the past, or from the present, but from the future they think they are going to live into.

An easy way of illustrating this would be to ask you to think of friends who hate their jobs. Notice how they light up on Friday afternoon. And then notice how they are on Monday morning (or even Sunday evening!).

Or think about the excitement that might attend being posted in your career to a new job role in a new country; an excitement that might not be there for your children, who can only see the friends they might lose from their past.

Or think about a divorce: a relationship between two people whose future has left them.

Or depression:

Depression is the inability to construct a future
Rollo May

One of the keys to living is to keep constructing a future – IN WORDS – that we can be excited by, and then aligning our behavior, as much as we can, with that.

Say it.
Then the action falls naturally out of that speaking.

And your past is only what readies you for creating the future

> *We all were sea-swallow'd, though some cast again*
> *(And by that destiny) to perform an act*
> *Whereof what's past is prologue; what to come,*
> *In yours and my discharge.*

W Shakespeare, *The Tempest*

The character who speaks these words is talking to a group of survivors of a ship-wreck ("sea-swallow'd"); he is reminding them that they could have died – and some of their colleagues did – but these lucky few have been given an almost miraculous opportunity to live again, to create a new life, albeit on a different island, far from a home they will probably never see again. All that is gone. It is in the past. It was wonderful to have had it. But now is the time to create ("discharge") a new future.

So, too, your past. Wonderful or horrible - that's always your story to tell - it is not coming back. You'll never have to deal with it again. Whether a depth of experiences to learn from, or, as Elbert Hubbard said about history, a litany of 'one damned thing after another', it is gone from you.

It is only a prologue to your future

'Life'. Transformed, in words, to *Living*.

Change *originally meant* to bend, shape

Authenticity *originally meant* to create, to increase

Culture *originally meant* to cultivate, to tend

Leadership *originally meant* to travel

Afford *originally meant* to advance

Engagement *originally meant* to promise

Work *originally meant* to create

And so on, and so on...

Isn't it amazing how many of these words are ACTIVE in their original sense? Verbs to be done rather than nouns to be experienced.

I can claim any word I speak and turn it into an action and then see where my power lies. It lies with me.

My language becomes source, my access to creation.

My words become my future.

And what could be more powerful in changing my world than that?

ABOUT THE AUTHOR

David Firth's coaching and consulting practice has its home in Colorado, USA and he also works internationally helping individuals and companies access the power of language and critical conversations.

Using his proprietary 'Bigger Futures' process, David works with businesses that want to build relationships with their stakeholders based on respect, commitment, accountability and mutuality.

David's writing and seminars focus on improving the work experience - enjoyment, satisfaction, meaning and engagement - for all levels of people in companies by shifting our relationship to ourselves, our work and our organizations. Most of all, he challenges the old story that "I would be happier or more effective if my boss were different".

His website is www.davidfirth.com

www.ingramcontent.com/pod-product-compliance
Lightning Source LLC
Chambersburg PA
CBHW031411040426
42444CB00005B/510